OF COLOR

McSWEENEY'S
SAN FRANCISCO

Copyright © 2020 Jaswinder Bolina

Cover by Jude Landry

McSweeney's and colophon are registered trademarks
of McSweeney's, a privately held company with wildly
fluctuating resources.

ISBN: 978-1-944211-86-8

10   9   8   7   6   5   4   3   2   1

www.mcsweeneys.net

Printed in Canada

OF COLOR

JASWINDER BOLINA

MᴄSWEENEY'S
SAN FRANCISCO

for Taran

CONTENTS

Empathy for the Devil 11

Writing Like a White Guy 21

Color Coded 41

What I Tell Them 57

The Writing Class 63

Foreign and Domestic 77

My People 85

American, Indian 91

White Wedding 107

Coda 127

Acknowledgments 131

I know someone could make a great weapon of me
if only I was thrown hard enough.

—Dean Young, "Tiger"

EMPATHY
FOR THE DEVIL

On September 13, 2001, a man I know tells me, "They should find the people that did this and shoot them in the street." He's a tawny-skinned immigrant a generation older than me, a naturalized U.S. citizen, and mostly a pacifist. There's a pause before he says, "But, you know, it's *amazing* what they did."

His gaze turns elsewhere. "For years," he adds, "these Americans and these British came into our countries and treated us like dogs. Now they know what the dogs can do to them."

Two days after Tuesday morning, he wants justice like an American, he aches like an American, but his perspective is stereoscopic. When he says, "They should find the people that did this," *they* means the U.S. government. When he says, "It's amazing what they did," *they* means the attackers. Both sides of the conflict are *they*. Neither is *we*.

He knows that he and I better resemble the photographs of the hijackers than we do the photographs of the firefighters, and when he says they "treated us like dogs," *us* means the Indian conflated with the Pakistani, the Pakistani mistaken for the Afghani, the Afghani called an Arab, the Arab undistinguished from the Persian and the Turk, the Shia and the Sunni and the Sikh all taken for one bearded and turbaned body. He means we who grew up in dusty villages in the Middle East and South Asia, who cooked outdoors by firelight and drank well water, whose lands were taken or who were taken from our land. He means the colonized, and from the perspective of the colonized, what the hijackers did *is* amazing: nineteen men departing within forty-five minutes of one another on four different flights from three different cities to devastate a nation thousands of miles and billions of dollars from the broke villages of the so-called Third World. When the immigrant says, "Now they know what the dogs can do to them," I find myself in the moat between us and them, where there's heroism in murder and murder in heroism.

I'm not certain I belong in that moat. Truth is, no imperialist ever made a dog of me. No colonist stole my tea leaves or plundered my oil well. No intelligence agency propped up a puppet regime to oppress, maim, or murder me. No matter whom I superficially resemble or how many English speakers my Sikh name confounds, I'm a citizen bankrolling an empire: a U.S. taxpayer, a voter, a part of the problem. I listen to the news every morning on NPR, read the BBC, the *Washington Post*, and the *New York Times* online, but I haven't been to Tunis. I don't know the boulevards of Benghazi, Cairo, or Islamabad. I know about the artillery and the bodies bleeding in the mosques of Homs, in the markets of Baghdad, and across Afghanistan, but I'm not so certain which factions or fighters or political parties want what and from whom. I'm a domestic in the heartland; when a body falls out there, it's a foreign body. Nobody ever trod on me.

On May 1, 2011, I'm sitting in a booth at the Hopleaf in Chicago when my phone buzzes. The bar offers over a hundred craft beers, a sedate clientele, and no television or internet, and for these reasons it's a perfect space to write in on a Sunday evening. The message on my phone states simply: "Osama bin Laden dead." It's from a friend in D.C. who works in the personnel office of the Obama administration, and it prompts me to gather my things and find a place with a live feed.

A block away, Simon's Tavern is silent for the broadcast of the president's statement from the East Wing. There's a brief cheer at his pronouncement, but the moment is uncanny. I can't imagine this feels anything like V-E Day or V-J Day. It certainly doesn't feel like the fall of the Berlin Wall, a memory still lucid from my childhood. It feels less like a moral victory than like witnessing an execution. Hitler had an army, Japan a navy, the Soviets a nuclear arsenal. Bin Laden lived twenty fugitive years in caves, tents, and dilapidated compounds. When I hear that he's dead, I don't feel anything resembling sorrow, but watching the young men in trees outside the White House waving flags and chanting *USA! USA!* I don't feel any kind of pride either. Both sides of the conflict seem barbaric. They killed one of them. Neither side includes me.

This doesn't mean I played no part. My role may be indirect, inadvertent, but to deny it would be a lie. I didn't endorse the kill order, but I voted for the man who did. My tax dollars paid, in part, for the bullets and the stealth helicopters. I might protest elements of U.S. foreign policy, but it's a policy written in my name. I've been told that my reservations about this are apologist, that to question America is a betrayal. I've been told that if I don't like it here, I should leave. But I do like it here, and I don't have anywhere else to go. I might be unwilling to accept the failings of the state, but I'm also unable to abandon it.

Besides, I don't disagree with the president's order, nor with its execution. *They should find the people that did this and shoot them in the street.* Ten years later, I can't say I object. I'm part of the problem I feel apart from.

On February 14, 2012, there's a girl on a unicycle on the sidewalk outside the Casa Nueva Cantina. She's wearing the brown leather jacket of a bombardier and wobbling past me up the easy slope of State Street. How effortless she makes it to indict her as a symbol of our excesses. How gleefully she rides through a world inhabited by tyrants conducting their manifold brutalities. Adorno says to write poetry after Auschwitz is barbaric. I'm oversimplifying what he means, but even the plain statement makes this girl on her unicycle seem monstrous. Ditto the hot-dog shack across the road, the tanning salon, the drunks in the barroom beside it. This is the view out a window in the heartland, a Wednesday night in Athens, Ohio. What a bore all our opulence is.

I'm tempted to vilify it, but my complicity in this culture makes the critique either self-righteous or hypocritical. Besides, I admire the girl's sense of whimsy. I wish I had a leather jacket, a hot dog, the skills to ride a unicycle. And I don't want to engage in easy liberalism, the activist mindset that contemplates, mourns, and criticizes but does nearly nothing to change the conditions that allow atrocity in the first place. Such a mindset might motivate me to vote left of center, to donate to Amnesty International. It might get me to march and to Occupy. But it operates at a safe distance, and that distance is part of the problem too. In that space, self-righteousness and cynicism fester. There every atrocity is born.

When we speak in the days that follow that second act of lethal efficiency—thirty or so commandos, one dog, two helicopters in alien airspace, a spectacular mission ending in under forty minutes with a bullet to bin Laden's eye—my friend expresses the same thing he did ten years earlier: he's amazed even as he understands.

In both cases, a man gave an order to kill and gave it for a reason. In both moments, that man viewed himself not as a murderer but as an executioner. Both delivered justice, and both employed a similar logic:

a. They came into our country and treated us like dogs.

b. We should find the people that did this and shoot them in the street.

c. Now they know what the dogs can do to them.

Thinking this way, the boys chanting *USA!* in the trees outside the White House on the first of May have arrived at the same conclusion as bin Laden and his cohort in the grainy video of their celebration on the eleventh of September. Both moments are reaction without recognition. I'm guilty of this too, my sense of alienation born of my inability to see myself fully in either side of the conflict. But the immigrant speaks across the moat between *us* and *them*, starkly voicing the contradictions that make up his perspective. His sense is one of empathy, which is born of an experience of the elsewhere, and the men in trees and the men in caves don't have enough of either. This is why they celebrate murder.

But when my friend says, "It's amazing what they did," he doesn't mean to praise any attack. There's nothing apologist about it either. He means that something in him recognizes a portion of every sorrow, a flash of every anger. He sees through both sides of the bullet hole. This is the amazing thing. And it may well offer our best rescue from alienation, apathy, and atrocity, from ourselves and each other.

WRITING LIKE
A WHITE GUY

My father says I should use a pseudonym. "They won't publish you if they see your name," he says. "They'll know you're not one of them. They'll know you're one of us." This has never occurred to me, at least not in a serious way. "No publisher in America's going to reject my poems because I have a foreign name," I answer. "Not in 2002."

In spite of my faith in the egalitarian attitude of editors, I understand where my father's coming from. I imagine him in England in 1965 with his beard shaved and his hair shorn, his turban undone and sent back to Bolina Doaba, Punjab—the town whose name we take as our own—a brown boy of eighteen become a Londoner. His circumstance must seem at once exhilarating and also like drifting in a lifeboat: necessary, interminable. I imagine the English of the era sporting an especially muted and disdainful brand of racism toward my alien father, his brother and sister-in-law, toward his sister and brother-in-law, his nieces and nephews, and the other Indians and Pakistanis they befriend on Nadine Street, Charlton, just east of Greenwich. The ache of exclusion arrives over every channel, dull and constant.

At least one realtor, a couple of bankers, and a few foremen have a different attitude. One white supervisor at the industrial bakery where my father labors invites him home for dinner. The Brit wants to offer an introduction to his single daughters. He knows my father's a hard worker, a trait so commonly attributed to the immigrant it sometimes seems a nationality unto itself, and maybe the quietude of the nonnative speaker appeals to the man's sense of decorum. He must find my father humble, upstanding, his sandy complexion indicative of a vigor exceeding that of the pale English suitors who have come calling. I picture my father's embarrassed but placid demeanor, his awkward formality in that setting, maybe charming the bashful, giggly daughters, impressing the supervisor even further. But nothing much comes of that evening. My father never visits again. He marries my mother, a Sikh Punjabi also, a few years later.

When he moves to hodgepodge Chicago nine years after he arrived in England, he becomes a denizen of this immigrant nation, its huddled masses. He might be forgiven for thinking he will not be excluded here, but he isn't so naïve. The U.S. in 1974 is its own version of the UK's insular empire, though the nature of the exclusion is different, is what we call *institutional*. My father knows that in the U.S. nobody should be rejected, not without some counterfeit of a reason, but all his nearly three decades as a machinist at the hydraulics plant near the airport teach him is that economies boom and economies bust, and if your name isn't Bill or Earl or Frank Malone you don't get promoted. You mind the machines. Bills and Earls supervise. Frank is the name the bosses go by, all of them hired after my father but raised higher. So, when my dad suggests I use a pseudonym, he's only steadying my two-wheeler, only keeping me from swimming too far out of the shallows at Foster Avenue Beach. It's only an extension of covering my college tuition, of paying my room and board.

At the time, I'm a year or so into an MFA. I stop by the office of a friend in my department, an older white poet. Publication feels impossible to me then, and the friend means to be encouraging when he says, "With a name like Jaswinder Bolina, you could publish plenty of poems right now if you wrote about the first-generation, minority stuff. What I admire is that you don't write that kind of poetry." He's right. I don't write that kind of poetry. To him, this is upstanding, correct, what a poet ought to do. It's indicative of a vigor exceeding that of other minority poets who have come calling. It turns out I'm a hard worker too. To his mind, embracing my difference would open editorial doors; that I don't, he admits, "will make it harder for you." When, a few months later, my father—who's never read my poems, whose fine but mostly functional command of English makes the diction and syntax of my work difficult to follow—tells me to use another name, he's encouraging also. He means: let them think you're a white guy. This will make it easier for you.

The thing I least believe about race in America is that we can disregard it. I'm nowhere close to alone in this, and yet the person I encounter far more often than the racist is the one who believes race isn't an active factor in her thinking, isn't an influence on his interactions with the racial other. Once, attending a panel discussion, I hear a professor of political philosophy explain that he never understood why the question in the U.S. is so often one of race, when in nearly every other industrialized nation on Earth the first conflict is one of class. He's Caribbean-born, with a doctorate from Canada, and it wasn't until he moved to the United States in the early 1970s, he says—about the same time my father arrived—that he fully understood this as a place where the continuing legacies of slavery and segregation force race and class into an unnatural codependency. It's why any claim that we can or should ignore color in this country is either a fanciful lie or a glad-handing con.

In his native land or my father's, where there prevails either relative homogeneity or a pervasive mingling of races, "minorities" are classed by status derived from any number of factors, of which race is rarely, if ever, principal. You can look down on anybody, even if they share your skin color, provided you have land enough, wealth enough, caste and education enough. It's only arriving in England that the Indian—who might not even recognize the descriptor *Indian*, preferring instead a regional or religious identity to a national one—realizes that anyone resembling him is subject to the derision of *coolie*. It's only in the U.S. that he discovers that, though he grew up far from any desert, his brown-skinned body can have a *sand nigger* or a *camel fucker* hurled at it from a passing car.

It's here that he learns that, though the first question remains one of class, the first American conflict is one of race, and that the nearer he is to whiteness, the nearer he is to wealth. If the racial other here aspires to equal socioeconomic footing, he has to work his way out of the categorical cul-de-sac that his name and appearance corral him into. The word we use for this process, *assimilation*, shares a Latin root with the word *similar*, implying that the outsider will be accepted simply by becoming more like his neighbors. But such becoming demands the negation of the old identity to make room for a new one, and, in this, assimilation is a destructive, rather than constructive, process. It isn't a come-as-you-are; it requires him to contort who he is into what someone else wants him to be.

So the tongue twists first. Any outsider's earliest and most essential effort at assimilation is in adopting and speaking the host country's language. What's unusual about the U.S. as a host country is that this is no less the case for the immigrant than for the native-born nonwhite. This is most obvious in the way African American vernacular language is variously described as *urban* (as in "of the slums of the inner city"), *street* (as in "of the gutter"), and *Ebonic* (as in "of ebony, of blackness"). Whatever this language is, these descriptors imply, it isn't English. Rather, it's *broken* English, which is also what we call the English of the non-European nonnative speaker.

It might seem both tempting and appropriate to categorize so-called "countrified" or "redneck" dialects the same way, except that proficiency in those dialects has helped multiple recent U.S. presidents and presidential candidates be viewed as more down-to-earth, more likable, rather than less well-spoken or intelligent. White vernaculars serve as evidence of charisma and folksiness, not ignorance. Not brokenness. In a country where class and race structurally overlap, then, what we call "standard" English becomes not the English of the educated or privileged classes but simply that of whiteness.

In 2007, the eventual vice president, campaigning against the eventual president, says, "I mean, you got the first mainstream African American who is articulate and bright and clean and a nice-looking guy. I mean, that's a storybook, man." Though the white candidate believes he's merely describing his opponent—with folksy generosity, at that—the description implies that the black man's appearance and eloquence contradict each other, that his adeptness with language is at odds with his blackness. Critics and rivals alike treat his eloquence as a novelty, which reminds voters that he isn't white. Conversely, because eloquence is bound in this country to white racial identity, some pundits begin asking, "But is he black enough?" The conundrum the candidate of color faces is that he must be an exceptional speaker and writer to succeed, but this quality will only allow others to regard him as an *exception* to his race. He is coerced into deciding whether to be a candidate or a black candidate. If he's the former, he can be accused of downplaying the issue of race opportunistically, of being a racial sellout. If he's the latter, making race a central argument for his candidacy, he will alienate too many white voters to win.

The poet of color faces a similar conundrum: will I be a writer or a minority writer? If I'm the former, adopting the English I'm taught in prep school, in college, in graduate school, I'm using a language assigned to somebody else while downplaying the issue of race. If I'm the latter, making race a central theme in my work, I risk alienating white readers or forcing myself into a niche where I can be disregarded as a novelty. I'm not making literature: I'm making *ethnic* literature.

* * *

The day I'm born, my father hands out cigars to the Bills and Earls and Franks of the factory floor, even though he has never smoked in his life. Smoking is anathema to his Sikh upbringing. Drinking, on the other hand, is not, and he gets gleefully and mercilessly drunk at home with his brother and friends. He boasts everywhere, "My son will be president." He believes it.

Twenty-four years later, when he counsels me to use a pseudonym, he knows I've already mastered the language. In spite of all his diligence and intelligence, this is a key he's never been given. I talk like them. I write like them. I'm an agile agent in the empire so long as nobody grows wise. He no longer expects a presidency, but he sees no limits to potential success in my chosen field, except for those placed on me by my racial difference. He doesn't consider the possibility that I write about race in my work, that I might want to embrace the subject, because he knows that I've been conditioned—like the candidate of black Kenyan and white Kansan bloodlines five years later—to resist making race the essential issue.

And it's true. The manner with which I avoid the subject in my first book is nearly dogmatic. I include binary code but not one word of Punjabi. My father makes an appearance, but only in the guise of a talking donkey. To acknowledge the many instances of racism he, my mother, or I have experienced would only underscore my otherness, which I fear will result in the same exclusions I experienced growing up in mostly white neighborhoods and schools. In those circumstances, assimilation isn't a political choice. Some atavistic survival instinct kicks in: when your numbers are few, you join the herd rather than resist it. To be racialized is to be marginalized. When another Asian kid joins the playground, we unwittingly vie to out-white each other.

When my father suggests I use a pseudonym, he knows he's suggesting I relinquish the name he and my mother gave me. This means relinquishing their son further to a culture that isn't their own, but I've never been kept from doing what the "American" kids do. (Though I was born here and my parents have long been citizens, "American" remains the descriptor my family uses to signify whiteness.) Like the Americans,

I join the Cub Scouts and play football at recess, attend birthday parties at classmates' houses and go to junior high socials. In high school, after years of elementary school mockery, I attempt, like the young Barry Obama, to anglicize my name to Jason. I go to the homecoming dance. I go to the prom. I stay out past curfew and grow my hair long. I insist that my mother close my bedroom door when she cooks so my clothes don't reek of cumin and turmeric. As I get older, I resist any suggestion that I study the sciences to prepare for a career in medicine or engineering. I never date an Indian girl; there are none in the philosophy and English departments I belong to anyway. My parents already know I'm bereft of their culture, that their son is almost as Frank or Bill as any other American, but they also believe this is necessary: that if their son is to become president, it won't happen while he's wearing a turban. They're willing to surrender their culture in order to assure my success, which means the price of my inclusion here is our alienation from each other.

* * *

As that political philosophy professor elucidated, it's because of the historical convergence of race and class in the U.S. that we associate the language of the educated, ruling classes with a particular racial identity. To decouple the two, as one might be able to do in a more racially homogenous country, is to realize that what's being described isn't the language of *whiteness* so much as the language of *privilege*—the privilege, in this case, of not needing to consider what others are forced to consider; of not needing to address questions of race, gender, sexuality, or class except by choice; of not needing to acknowledge wherefrom one speaks and instead professing to speak from a blank slate. It's the position of no position, the voice from nowhere or from everywhere, and in this it is Godlike.

To the poet, though, the first question isn't one of class or color. The first question is one of language. Poetry, as Mallarmé famously told the hapless would-be poet Edgar Degas, is made of words, not ideas. And yet for the poet of color or the female poet, for the gay or transgender poet, even for the white male poet born outside of socioeconomic privilege, a difficult question arises: whose language do we use? Our academic and cultural institutions, along with their literary canon and its language, have historically been the possessions of a largely wealthy, heteronormative male whiteness. Writers who aren't those things, if they are to enter the academy and its canon, are asked to assimilate into diction, syntax, and grammar that don't coincide with perceptions of their identities. They are asked to deracialize, desexualize, un-gender, and un-class their language at the outset, and promised that the better they approximate whiteness in so doing, the nearer they'll be to a universal art.

This isn't to say minority poets aren't permitted to bring alternative vernaculars into our work. Our literary language has expanded at the insistence of white poets, from Wordsworth to O'Hara, in their calls to incorporate colloquial language into poetry. Since then, the monolith of the canon has been slowly eroded by vernaculars of color as deployed by the Harlem Renaissance, the Black Arts Movement, Cave Canem, VONA, Kundiman, and others. But even heeding O'Hara's or Wordsworth's calls, I'm left in an awkward position: I don't possess any

English significantly different from plain old overeducated Midwestern English. In my writing, I have only the parlance of whiteness to express my brownness. The parlance of privilege.

In the forty-six years since my father left Punjab, the forty-odd years since my mother left also, my parents clambered up the socioeconomic ladder with reasonable middle-class success. We weren't exactly wealthy, but I did wind up in private school instead of the public high, only isolating me further from those whose racial identity I shared. At university, my parents' successes permitted me to study the subjects I wanted to study rather than those that might have guaranteed future wealth. I didn't need to become a doctor or a lawyer to support the clan. I got to major in philosophy and later attend graduate school in creative writing. Through all of this, though I experienced occasional bigotry on the street, and though I was often one of only two or three students of color in my program, my racial identity was mostly overlooked or disregarded. I became so adept in the language and culture of the academy that on more than one occasion a colleague told me, "I don't think of you as a minority." Or, as a cousin who's known me since infancy says, mostly joking, "You're not a minority. You're just a white guy with a tan."

What she means is that my assimilation is complete, that a reader who encounters my work without knowing my name or seeing my picture might not be faulted for assigning the poems a white racial identity. This is a product of my language, which is a product of my education, which is a product of the privilege afforded by my parents' successes. The product of all these factors together is that the writing, this essay included, can't seem to help sounding *white*. And still, my cousin can't be correct. Race is too essential to the American experience to ever be truly overlooked. I can no more write as a white guy than I can pick my skin color. I'm not sure where this leaves me.

Invited to give a few readings at a literary festival in a rural part of the country, I borrow my father's compact SUV and let its GPS guide me for a few days. I spend afternoons and evenings reading poems with local and visiting writers at community centers and public libraries. The audiences are largely kind, white-haired, white-skinned locals enthusiastic to listen to us speak about our work, even when they've never heard of us. During the introductions before each event, even the organizers who invited me have difficulty getting my name right. In one school library, I enunciate it over and again: *Jas* as in the first part of *justice*; *win* as in the opposite of defeat; *der*, which rhymes with *err*, meaning to be mistaken. "JasWINder," I say, lilting the second syllable, and smile as a dozen audience members mouth each syllable along with me. When they feel they have it right, they grin broadly.

After each event, I chat with them one or two at a time, doing my best to reflect their warmth. In town after town, though, while signing a book or shaking a hand, I get some variation on the same recurring question. No one delivers it better, with so much beaming neighborliness and unwitting irony, than the woman who says she enjoyed my poems very much and then asks, admiringly, "You're so Americanized, what nationality are you?"

She doesn't hear the tiredness in my reply: I was born and raised in Chicago, but my parents are from northern India. I ought to be offended, but I'm not, not really. Hers is an expression of curiosity born of genuine interest rather than of sideshow spectacle. I'm the only nonwhite writer at the events. I'm the only one who gets this question. I bristle, but I understand where she's coming from.

After my brief tour is over, I drive the five hundred miles back to suburban Chicago to return the Toyota. I eat dinner at home, and afterward my father drops me in the city. Invariably, the trip down the Kennedy Expressway toward the skyline makes him nostalgic for his underpaid days in small apartments on the North Side, his city long before it became my city. We talk as usual about the news, politics, the family. When he remembers to ask how my poetry trip went, I say the audiences were kind and the drives long. Out there, I say, the country looks like a painting of itself. I don't tell him what the woman asked, the question echoed by others. It won't matter that she asked it while eagerly shaking my hand. It won't matter that she offered her gratitude that I'd come all that way to read in her hamlet on the outskirts of America. It won't matter that she meant the opposite: he'll only hear the question as the old exclusions come aching again, as confirmation that this country will not accept us as part of itself. But I don't feel excluded so much as I do fatigued. By whiteness, by brownness, by all of race altogether.

I'd rather not think about it at all. I'd rather not write that kind of poetry, that kind of anything. Yet in poems and in essays and in books to come, I will write about it. Race will come to define me even when I attempt to avoid it because of the way our evasions always come to define the contours of our fixations. Because of the way color has come to define this country. I never can write like a white guy. I can only be a brown guy making a study of a life in language, whatever language I best possess. And though my language might once have belonged exclusively to white men, to a culture of exclusion, I can deploy and alter it now in ways they couldn't have imagined. When I write, the language belongs to me.

COLOR CODED

When the blonde girl shouted, "Hey!" and ran over to stop my bicycle, a voltage of hope charged through my twelve-year-old body. No blonde girl had ever stopped me in all the years I'd ridden down the lane between the park district playground and rows of suburban townhouses. No blonde girl had ever stopped me anywhere. I thought she might want to know my name. Maybe we'd walk across the way to sit on the park swings. It was 1990. I'd never kissed a girl. This might be love. As I settled to a stop, she landed her hands on mine, squeezed, looked me straight in the face, and with grave seriousness asked, "Are you a Hindu or a Gandhi?"

Her mouth broke into a sneer before she released me and ran back to a gallery of cackling friends, their laughter chasing me down the lane past the cracked expanse of the tennis courts to the quiet of the comics shop a mile or so away. This wasn't the worst thing anyone had ever said to me. By twelve, I'd taken plenty of slurs. But this encounter was a total non sequitur, both gratuitous and nonsensical. *Gandhi* is a name, not an epithet. My family isn't Hindu; even if we were, I'm not sure how being described as such would be an insult.

To dismiss this episode as an artifact of adolescent daftness would be to ignore the sophistication in the blonde girl's behavior. She deduced my family's national origin, elaborated upon her deduction by identifying that nation's foremost religious majority, and further recognized one of its preeminent founding fathers—all from the sight of my face. Impressive for a kid who might otherwise be dismissed as ignorant. She wasn't ignorant. She was making inferences, some of them quite clever.

But she also deliberately ignored any complexity in me, any possibility that I might be someone other than I appeared to be. She took the upper hand by erasing any possibility of sophistication in her target. Ignorance can be forgiven. It was the willfulness of her act that made it deplorable.

I didn't set out that afternoon thinking how brown I was, how anyone might assault me with that fact. My encounter with the blonde girl felt like getting horse-collared. The effect of this kind of diminishment is profound, the ensuing humiliation automatic. It isn't rooted in shame. I don't remember regretting myself or wanting to disavow my family and the genetics that made me. I liked who I was. But I felt futile, my embarrassment born of powerlessness. I spent days—years, even—thinking about what I should've said, with what ferocity of wit and logic I might have shut her down. But I didn't shut anybody down. I ran.

I might have escaped her cruelty in the moment, but I internalized my shame over running for a long time after. I told myself I'd do better next time. Next time I'd flank and maneuver. But one next time, early on a college evening in 1997 while I was walking down South Michigan Avenue, a pair of red-faced, middle-aged white men in a Jeep Grand Cherokee slowed to ask if I was a camel fucker. The passenger lunged for my arm and I pulled it away, a frightened child again. Another next time, a few weeks after 9/11, a white guy stopped his pickup truck to block my path through an Ann Arbor crosswalk. He stared me down until I knew I was something other than an MFA student. I shaved my grunge-era-holdover beard the next morning. Another next time, a few years later, a white guy hollered "sand nigger" at me from a car passing so fast I didn't have time to react. He gave not one shit for my doctorate, for my first book of poems or the next one. I took to wearing headphones everywhere I went. I avoided eye contact with anyone passing. I didn't realize then, after these and so many other incidents I won't bother to recount, how invisible I attempted to become.

Still, the TSA sees me. The neighborhood watch sees me. The police see me. Their way of seeing is deemed necessary, not racist but defensible per the procedural-sounding label *racial profiling*. They're making inferences. Justifiable inferences, allegedly, but they don't feel very different from the others I remember, each one founded on incorrect assumptions and active decisions to ignore certain particulars about my identity. Except now I'm no longer the butt of an adolescent joke. Now such inferences might mistake me for a threat, my selfhood erased by the semiautomatic suspicion that I am something other than an "ordinary" citizen. This kind of suspicion can get a body detained or arrested, can get a body killed. In this context, I feel obliged to demonstrate my normalcy, my loyalty—my docility, even—which is a strange reaction from a person on the receiving end of unprovoked aggressions. I become the victim apologetic.

This isn't fair, but it turns out the world isn't as objective as all those college philosophy classes suggested. It values and devalues me, which alters the way I behave and in turn the way I see myself. This is how race comes to affect an entire ontology, how it becomes metaphysical. I possess a version of who I am that feels internally consistent and authentic, but that identity is rejected by others for little more than the bone structure of my face, for a trick of light refracting through the melanin in my epidermis. When you're affected by this kind of prejudice, it isn't the individual act that matters. It's the lesson offered by all such acts taken together, by their sheer pervasiveness and the oppressive regularity with which they afflict people of color around you. You start out an American kid on your bicycle until someone hollers for you to go back to your country; until security follows you through the store, the airlines kick you off your flight, the politician vows to remove you from your home; until the patriot punches you in the face or the police strangle or shoot you.

Firsthand experience of racism is the kind of thing a poet probably ought to write about. But the first time I wrote a poem about it, a white poet lamented that I was merely outing the obvious, only reiterating something he, I, and many readers of poetry already knew was wrong. As notable anti-Semite Ezra Pound declared long ago, the artist's central task is to *make it new*. The white poet's complaint was that, though my poem may have been well-written, even publishable, it hadn't made racism new.

I don't altogether disagree—I've taken Pound's dictum to heart as much as any other poet—but we need to be clearer about exactly what *new* means, whether it refers to innovations of form, of content, or of both. What the white poet missed is that the observation of racial injustice is itself new, that it hasn't existed in poetry for very long or been explored to anything approaching completion. For those unaffected by racism—or sexism, homophobia, transphobia, or so many other intolerances—maybe every account of victimization blends together. You might be sympathetic to the cause of racial parity, but your disconnection from the actual experience of racial disparity leads you to support the cause without being especially interested in specific accounts of it. You might feel that racism is racism, each particular part of the same continuous subject. You don't need another poem describing how awful it is. You want something *new*.

This is how race and racism come to be seen as passé subjects for poetry, subjects that are already too familiar or too personal or somehow lesser than other, more universal ones. When this occurs—and it does, with surprising frequency—the argument is often based on the logic that most poems in our anthologies are devoid of racial or ethnic subject matter. It might posit that Keats's odes aren't especially interested in race, but rather in beauty and truth. That, in spite of ample evidence to the contrary, J. Alfred Prufrock isn't a vehicle for the aging T.S. Eliot to lament his diminished sex appeal but the rumination of a Modernist observer alienated by the urban wasteland and the urbane women drifting through it. These paragons of the poetic canon are laudable, the argument goes, not for their confessions of private experience but for their advancements of form. Their subject is the "human" condition, and their work is novel for the way it constructs and deconstructs that subject.

But if neither Keats nor Eliot nor Pound ever wrote from or about their experiences of racial identity, it is almost certainly because that identity was never noted or challenged by anyone around them. For this reason, though I find plenty of pleasure and insight in their poems, I can't say they're more *objective* or *universal* than a Langston Hughes meditation on a brass spittoon, or an Agha Shahid Ali ghazal remembering Kashmir, or a Natasha Trethewey recollection of her hair being painfully straightened with hot combs. Race doesn't affect Keats's ontology or Eliot's or Pound's, the metaphysic that underlies their artistry, the way it affects Hughes's or Ali's or Trethewey's or mine or that of so many others. The white masters, masters though they may be, are oblivious to those experiences of bigotry and exclusion that are condemnably common for the rest of us. In this essential matter, those writers of the literary canon are utterly ignorant, and so their reports on the human condition are gapingly incomplete. And still there are critics who argue that lyricism is a finished thing, that a white account of the self is a sufficiently universal contemplation, that any emphasis on race will only diminish its universality.

This is where our confusion about Pound's dictum has landed us. *Make it new* is predicated upon a version of literary history that sees poetry as a kind of progress:

the Early Modern begets the Romantic begets the Modern begets the Postmodern. This view implies that poetry advances by making continuous improvements upon itself, which is as wrongheaded as understanding biological evolution as the improvement of a species toward a perfect endpoint. Worse, to commit to a normative and linear history of poetry allows for the dismissal of any writing that doesn't continue, and thus implicitly endorse, that history. Any poem that isn't *new* relative to long-held beliefs about the old—that certain canonical poems are universal in their perspectives, for instance, or that the confessional speaker is distinct from and lesser than the philosophical lyric speaker—is readily disregarded. The *new* remains under the jurisdiction of whoever controlled the old, and no minorities need apply.

But there isn't progress in poetry. There's only an art form adapting to the manifold pressures culture and moment exert upon each of us as poets. Better, then, to accept the evolutionary model of natural selection and understand that when context changes, our writing responds. Sometimes formerly dominant perspectives are selected out. Sometimes vestigial styles are selected back in. Complaining doesn't help, no matter how knowledgably the complainants ground themselves in a history of the art. Doing so is like asking a parrot to turn itself into a dinosaur, or claiming that returning to the geopolitics of the 1950s will make America great again. The tectonics shifted. The asteroid struck. That America is over.

And now, as a literature of color, of gender, and of sexuality begins to assert itself at long last, there are those who argue that the fact of such variables gives minority writers a new and undue competitive advantage; that writers who discuss race in their work are beneficiaries of tokenism, itself a consequence of the political correctness and affirmative actions that undermine meritocracy in publishing and leave white writers dispossessed; that a history of racism has given way to a new era of "reverse racism." This critique came to the fore in 2015 when, admitting he had been duped by Michael Derrick Hudson's publication of a poem under the pen name Yi-Fen Chou, Sherman Alexie—who had included the poem in that year's edition of *Best American Poetry*—copped to what he called "racial nepotism." His admiration for the piece, he explained, was in part based on the idea that it concerned subject matter he hadn't expected someone named Yi-Fen Chou to write about. That is, Alexie meant to reward a Chinese writer for avoiding anything discernibly Chinese in her writing, as if the avoidance were an accomplishment worth celebrating.

I believe fully that writers of color should address whatever subjects enthrall us, and that there is much to treasure and learn about race even when it isn't an explicit subject in our art. But Alexie's reasoning not only undermines the possibility that nonwhite concerns can be Western, much less universal; it also places an outsized burden on writers of color by holding a higher esteem for those who *don't* write their own experience, for poetry that remains silent on race or ethnicity. In selecting the poem for the reasons he did, Alexie didn't commit racism against whiteness so much as engage in the same preference for conventional, deracialized,

Eurocentric subject matter that white people have long favored—which is to say he committed good old-fashioned regular racism.

For his part, Hudson's use of a Chinese woman's name had nothing to do with the experience of any actual Yi-Fen Chou. He merely took a poem he had written and attributed it to someone else. In this, he wasn't guilty of cultural appropriation but guilty of something far more perverse: wearing someone else's skin for his own gratification, for the hope of cadging some modestly increased notoriety. A white man using a fabricated racial identity where he believes it offers an advantage isn't dispossession. It's a choice. It's an engagement with race that is entirely elective. This is what gets elided by those who cite so-called reverse racism for their failure to land this job or win that award: they can choose to ignore race when they succeed, and choose to blame it when they fail. The real, living woman whose identity, subjectivity, and autonomy Hudson thieved in service of his self-interests could never be granted the same liberty—not in a country where so many would-be standard-bearers are eager to dismiss her every achievement as a product of affirmative action and celebrate any failing as evidence of her inferiority.

Losing out where your forebears always won doesn't mean you're a victim. It means, again, that the context has changed. Other people get a shot now too. And yet the laments only seem to be growing louder on talk radio, on Fox News, at political rallies, even in the generally polite and progressive company of poets. Shifting demographics are cited as evidence of the continued diminishment of white thriving. The arrival of minorities where they haven't been permitted or expected before—in the White House, on television, in literary journals, at book award ceremonies—are framed as coming at the expense of white achievement. But the losses of one white person, or even of several white people, don't represent the losses of all white people. To see evidence of a systemic conspiracy in a person of color's ascension to any position once held exclusively by white people, exclusively for white people, is to mistake the outlier for the system. Rather than acknowledging my experiences of racist abuse or anyone else's, rather than confronting the real threats people of color in this country face daily, the claim to reverse racism creates a false equivalency between subjugation and inconvenience.

But none of that lousy accounting can take my memory of the blonde girl away from me. No politics of paranoia can eclipse my actual anxiety walking down the street, my actual unease in the airport, my actual fear driving through entire regions of this country. No empty gesture at inclusion can allay the fears so many people of color have of the police, of the criminal justice system, of their fellow citizens openly, proudly seeking to make America what it once was. Those fears are founded on experience, not inference. Those experiences are as real as our national legacies of slavery and segregation, of ghettoization and internment and deportation. Of murder. No demagogue can erase these. No tokenism can correct them. No pundit and no poet should minimize or dismiss them. No white gripe can conceal the fact that that pain, that violence, and that shame are also America.

WHAT I TELL THEM

I 'd like to tell them there are too many poets. I'd like to tell them we don't need any more and don't need any more competition. Too many throbbing bodies, not enough room in the bed. I'd like to tell them, you should go to other departments. You should go to the other departments and become exquisite bankers your future in-laws will favor. You matter too little, and anyway, there isn't any place for poetry. You know too little, what are you doing here?

I don't say these things, though I think sometimes I should. I don't say them because I've seen photographs of Lascaux, so instead I say, Let me tell you about Lascaux and how you and art are irrepressible. I feel wise when I say this, though I'm only twelve or so years removed from where they are now, and I know too little. I tell them this too. I say, I'm only twelve or so years removed from where you are, and I know too little.

Then there are other things, invented and borrowed, I go ahead and tell them, things I'd like to say in French or in Latin or very cryptically in English as though I'm under incredible strain: you don't matter; only the poem matters. Or: poems aren't made of ideas, they're made of words. Or: you don't have to be honest, but you gotta be sincere. I don't say any of it in French or in Latin because I never learned enough French or Latin. I don't render it cryptic. I say these things directly because I believe they're true. It's true, I worry I sound didactic or woefully earnest and have embarrassed myself, but then irony would be easier than earnestness, and anyway, this isn't about me. Only the poems matter.

I tell them, you are rare people for whom poems matter but, even so, only so rare. After all, I tell them, everybody writes poetry. All of us, in our sentimental, self-important scrawl in blank hardback journals bought from the rack next to the register at the bookstore. I have those journals too. They're in a box under the folding table I use for a desk. I take them out every so often and, embarrassed, tear out a few pages. Entire books eventually disappear. Everyone writes poetry, I tell them, which is why there's a place for it, and you have these journals too, but you're rare people for going public with this information.

I tell them, by going public with this information, you agree to the term and condition that your poetry is no longer your own. Sure, we talk to ourselves, we write notes to ourselves, but no one writes poetry to himself, herself, themself, oneself. You might write *for* yourself, but you write *to* somebody else. You should be nice to that person. That person is seated beside you. Say hello.

But this person isn't enough. You want somebody else. I tell them, you want the somebody who would stroll into a library in Tucson or Greenwich on a Wednesday and find what you've written. You want that person to pull you down off a shelf in the future and open you up and marvel. You want to be somebody's afternoon reading on the veranda, somebody's xerox hung with a tack on their inspiration wall.

I tell them that much is possible, but what you write here won't appear in the *Norton*. No editor will call you. For that sort of thing to happen, you have to walk into a library, open a book of poems, and marvel. You have to do this several times a month—several times a week if you can—over many years. You'll need to paper your wall.

What you write between treks to the library will disappear under the folding table, and you'll reach for it every so often and, embarrassed, discard a few pages until entire books disappear. Some of it, though, you'll keep, and some of it might find a way to a shelf and to somebody else. That much is possible, I tell them. Some of it will congeal and assemble.

I tell them the trick is entirely in language. Poems are made of words, and these words need to be your own. Your words are what sincerity is made from, I tell them, and in this you have all you need for poetry. I tell them, use the words you remember from cartoons, words from your mother speaking of rutabaga, from your chemistry tutor and the redhead who at first ignored you, the words you think of when you think of the bodega on Granville and yourself, later, naked in the redhead's apartment. These words are yours, and your poems should be made out of them.

I give them examples. I tell them, our 'morning' is always 'frigid' and 'gray,' our 'clothing' is always 'ragged' and 'torn,' and our 'fingers' are always 'stained' 'with' 'tobacco,' 'the' 'fingers' 'of' 'smoke' 'caressing' 'the' 'light bulb.'

I tell them, your morning should be *neurons* and *steam*. You should arrive in a *smock* or in *machinist's regalia*. You needn't bother with smoking and fingers, we've had enough cigarettes in poetry. Your words need to supplant our words so we can arrive at knowledge and also discover we know too little. It will be startling.

Your task is to arrange these words strangely in order to explain what happened more clearly. Your task is to help us understand what happened, I tell them, but what happened isn't always simply the facts. What happened isn't always a story. Sometimes it's just some images. Sometimes it's entirely sound.

To figure out which it is, I tell them, you'll need to let the poem overthrow you. It's made of words, and even if they're your words, they're part of language, and language is much bigger than you. Naturally, this will generate some conflict. The poem will sometimes need to be silent where you want to speak, or be explicit where you would turn to muttering. It will be confused about what you know for certain or certain about what confuses you. Sometimes the poem will sputter and quit no matter how hard you admire or kick it. Sometimes it neglects you completely, and this, I tell them, is okay. You're here to relinquish, I tell them. You're here to sever a nerve.

THE WRITING CLASS

S ometime in the early seventies, my parents got into a still-infamous row after one of them spent two dollars on a houseplant the other insisted they couldn't afford. That spat took place a few years before I was born, but they've laughed about it so often I almost remember being there. It fits into my real memories of other squabbles they had in our shabby apartment on the north side of Chicago, the worn green carpet in its kitchen, the claw-foot tub with no shower in its single bathroom, the scuffed paint on its walls, their arguments tumbling through whole evenings. It fits into my memory of what money meant to their otherwise happy marriage. Sundays we'd go in the used Montego from one market with a sale on tomatoes to the other, where a gallon of milk sold for ten cents cheaper. On the way home, we'd forgo the bright new gas station for the gloomy old one where the unleaded cost a few cents less.

These are some of the ways my immigrant parents survived recessions, layoffs, and the disappearance of entire industries from the U.S. economy. This is how they earned, saved, and invested enough to move us into a brick split-level house in the suburbs with a two-and-a-half-car garage by the time I started secondary school. Though my father kept clocking in at the same hydraulics plant while my mother entered data for an hourly wage at a financial publishing company, they could afford to buy me a set of encyclopedias and an Apple IIGS. They could pay for park district tennis lessons and a stereo with a CD player and a dual cassette deck. They could send me to the private academy instead of the public high school. This is how I lived a socioeconomic reality almost entirely separate from theirs.

While my parents scrimped and stressed daily as part of the working classes, I went to a school with honor societies, AP courses, and study abroad programs. I went to college. I parlayed my philosophy major into a high-paying job at a software startup south of Silicon Valley, then, after less than six months, decided to apply to MFA programs in creative writing. This didn't make sense to my parents. Though we were far removed from the ragged apartments of my childhood, their class consciousness, still rooted in those earlier struggles, told them we weren't the kind of people who did certain things. Abandoning a salaried job with stock options for a graduate degree offering little hope of future employment or reliable income was chief among these. But I liked the integrity in my plan. If a degree in poetry dumped me into bohemian impoverishment, I thought, so be it. At least I was earnest in my pursuit. I was that kind of people.

My father wrote his share of poems in high school in India. He still recites verses, though never his own, in

Punjabi on occasional late evenings. My mother, the daughter of a schoolteacher and top of her high school class in a village fifty miles or so from my father's, could probably recite a few herself. Poetry wasn't a bad idea to either of them, in the abstract—it might even be a noble pursuit. But it also seemed a thing better left to the children of the wealthy than to the son of working-class immigrants. To their minds, being a poet wasn't a *job*. They still felt too near the keen edge of hardship to see me follow so precarious a path. I didn't see the danger.

I don't think I entirely understood that it was the economic advantage they had worked and paid for that permitted me to be so brazen. If I'd been anything other than a protected spectator during my parents' lean years, if I hadn't had their income and savings for a safety net during and after college, I probably would have stuck it out at that startup or some other bleary office job. Economists and accountants distinguish class based on objective metrics such as net worth or income, but class consciousness would be better defined by the kinds of choices we feel permitted to make. Where the working classes are forced to act out of necessity, the privileged are allowed to act on desire. My parents' money, modest as it was and still is, did more than pay for the things I needed. It allowed me to want things they couldn't afford to want themselves.

I believed my dream of a life in poetry to be pure, uncontaminated by socioeconomics. My concerns were artistic concerns, I thought, my acceptance of bohemianism an earnest embrace of the artist's life. The contradiction is that those concerns, however sincere, led me to graduate school. The desire to write and publish poetry leads a lot of us there, which is all well and good, but there's nothing bohemian about it. On the contrary, those of us who are able to attend grad school can do so only as beneficiaries of structural advantages that separate us from people like my parents who might appreciate poetry but lack the time and resources to spend on a purpose-built education in it. If there's a problem with this, it's that literature is an art, which means it should at least attempt to represent the society in which it's produced. It can't fully do that if its primary mode and conditions of production exclude most of the population.

* * *

I wanted to write poetry. I didn't need a graduate degree to do this. Nobody does. But graduate degree programs in creative writing offer a two- to five-year respite from that other life working long hours in restaurants, bars, factories, or offices. We're given time and money, no matter how brief and how paltry, to focus almost exclusively on our obsessions—no small advantage over everyone writing on the fringes of a forty-plus-hour workweek. That advantage is often supplemented along the way by financial support from parents, partners, and spouses. Not to neglect the fact that we know such programs exist in the first place, that we possess the credentials and resources to apply and enroll. Every would-be grad student needs a college degree, letters from qualified recommenders, access to qualifying exams like the GRE, and funds to cover application fees. We need a flexible share of time to spend on years away from gainful employment and, for many of us, a safety net if we fail to find gainful employment afterward.

While some aspiring writers from less privileged backgrounds do find their way to graduate school, they remain substantially outnumbered. Because socioeconomic disparities in the U.S. have long coincided with gender and race, class goes a long way in determining the demographic makeup of grad programs, which has far-reaching consequences for who gets represented in an American literary canon increasingly dominated by graduate-schooled writers. Even if we believe demographic trends have improved since my time as an MFA student almost two decades ago, this doesn't mean the system is correcting its culture of privilege. Instead, I worry, more of us are simply being indoctrinated into it.

The more advanced our degree, the more conversant we become in the mores of the upper classes. For creative writing programs, this is borne out in wine and cheese receptions, in the pomp and circumstance of the formal reading series, and in the annual pageant of the AWP (Association of Writers & Writing Programs) conference, where thousands of nattily dressed writers convene to network, present, and perform in the hotel ballrooms of America's priciest urban centers, sleeping four to a room and putting ten-dollar drinks in the lobby bar on already overburdened credit cards. If grad school's pay scale—which trumpeted a stipend of fourteen thousand dollars a year as desirable, if not enviable, when I enrolled—provides an authentic experience of lean living, its culture delivers the distinct whiff of old-money society.

And when entry into a field becomes contingent upon class advantage, when participation in it becomes a kind of class indoctrination, stratifications are inevitable. Those of us who matriculate through MA, MFA, and PhD programs join a select club set apart from the general population: writers who can make some kind of living, no matter how meager, from work related to their art. Access to this club is so limited, and our numbers so few, that we become a class unto ourselves, a writing class modeling poetry's own version of a 1 percent.

Not that the club is so decadent as the analogy implies. I put in time after my MFA, and again after my PhD, earning lousy incomes as an adjunct lecturer, postdoctoral fellow, and visiting writer. I taught overwhelming course loads for underwhelming pay with no health insurance or job security. Still, I remained a poet in the academy, party to its culture even as it exploited me as a low-cost laborer. Though I lived a version of the bohemian lifestyle I'd romanticized when I decided to try for an MFA, a lifestyle resembling the one I'd been born into and raised out of by my parents, off I'd go to every wine and cheese reception as though my learning and art somehow distinguished me from anyone working in a factory or a Walmart earning as little as I did.

Earning as little as I did, I came to understand that it isn't our learning that distinguishes the classes from one another so much as it is the affects we acquire, the way we come to speak and sound. I can't imagine the wealthy often say *WIC check* or *second shift*, just as the poor probably don't much use words like *escrow* or *dividends*. For the middle classes, there might be a dissertation to be had in studying the diction of our Facebook posts as a function of income—picture a line graph where x is annual salary and y is occurrences of the words *resort* or *reception* or, for that matter, *dissertation*. The thousands of choices we make in our daily vernacular are almost entirely reflexive, and we hardly notice them at all when talking or writing to people who speak like us. If we encounter only those people, if nobody comes along to challenge our language and its embedded frames of reference, ours becomes a private conversation, continually reaffirming our existing perspectives.

For poets, this is downright existential. The practice of poetry should be utterly antithetical to any kind of linguistic restriction. The entire premise of writing, the thing that fuels and continually renews it, is that it demands the expansion of language. We can, again, achieve such expansion with a library card instead of an advanced degree, but that's not what many of us do. We go to graduate school, and we believe we're doing so for the way it will benefit our writing. We're not. We're doing it for the money, at least the dream of pocketing some of it.

Poetry isn't a job, but in 2001, when I started my MFA, it seemed like it could be. The steady growth of MFA programs nationally throughout the eighties and nineties was predicated on the idea that this was a terminal degree offering the real chance of an income at its terminus: you published your poems, then you published a book, then you went out and landed a tenure-track gig at another university. The MFA was the aesthete's version of a DDS. Had I known the realities of the academic job market at the outset, I might have run screaming to dental school, but I didn't. I went to poetry school, and I did so as much for a job as for my writing.

I don't fault myself, or anyone else, for attempting to make a career out of a passion. But in the past quarter century that careerism, shared by thousands of us, has propelled poetry in the U.S. through its own version of an industrial revolution. In 2019, a *Poets & Writers* database listed nearly four hundred small presses that publish one or more books of poetry a year; it would be difficult even to estimate the number of print and digital outlets that publish individual poems daily, weekly, monthly, annually, but *P&W* puts it at over eleven hundred. All of these presses and journals are housed, along with our graduate schools, under the umbrella of the AWP, which in less than three decades has grown into an industrial complex complete with commercial and boutique brands, gatekeepers and cliques, infighting and nepotism.

What was for centuries a small-scale pursuit available mostly to white men of means, then, has become a cottage industry attended by thousands of established and aspiring writers. In principle, this is a good thing. Yet there doesn't seem to be much demand for the growing supply of writing produced by graduate-schooled poets on the part of anyone other than graduate-schooled poets. Our writing creates its own economy. And when the consumers of poetry are almost exclusively also those who produce it, we are left ascribing value to our own product. The trouble is that nobody outside the industry needs to agree with our valuations.

And if the critics are right, nobody does. Poetry has been slammed in *Harper's*. It's been declared dead by the *Washington Post* and called AWOL on NPR. When observers announce poetry's demise, they cite impalement by ivory tower. They tell us poetry is out of touch, that it's too entangled in the incestuous relationship among graduate creative writing programs, literary journals, and publishers; that this has marginalized what was once a mainstream art and disconnected it from those masses apparently clamoring for poetry out there in the wide world. Yet those masses clamor still, turning to singer-songwriters, rap artists, Instagram poets, slams, and open-mic nights for reflections of the world in verse. The real complaint by poetry's eulogists is that too few in that vast audience ever turn to us certified, credentialed, bona fide poets. Our poems have become a thing like that two-dollar houseplant my parents waged their small battle over. Neither is an object anybody needs. Both can be ignored when more urgent concerns come along.

It's entirely possible that more people are writing, reading, performing, and publishing poetry today than at any other point in human history. If we want that poetry to matter to people outside our classrooms and conference halls, if we want to bring the masses to our work, then their lives and their languages need to matter to us first. We need to learn as much about WIC checks and second shifts as we do about disjunctive narrativity and postmodernism, not out of a desire for a larger audience but for the sake of our art and its future. The only true job of the poet is to destabilize and expand language. This is how poetry changes the world: by the plodding, unending effort of all of us to alter line by line, phrase by phrase, word by word, the way we describe ourselves and everything we encounter. We can't do this while isolated by privilege. If our work doesn't bring refreshment to readers outside of our industry, if too many feel disconnected from it, it's probably not because their desire for the poetic has gone unmet or gone away altogether, but because they can't afford our version of it.

FOREIGN AND DOMESTIC

On my knees in stone mulch at 1 a.m., my hands raised predictably above my head, my back to the three boys relieving me of my wallet and phone and laptop bag, and one of them has a taser to my neck and another maybe a gun, I can't help but marvel at how nice this neighborhood is. The two-story, midcentury condos in front of which I'm being mugged for the first time in my life are nestled around a courtyard's thicket of palms. They list for upward of $250K, though they're short on square footage and ripe for renovation, and the newer-construction townhouses down the sidewalk run upward of $850K. A canopy of royal poinciana glows Crayola green in the white streetlight over the wide boulevard. A row of Mercedes E-Classes and Range Rovers glitter along the curb. Even the distant bass rhythm of a band playing blocks away only deepens the calm. Location being the meat of good realty, I'm almost proud to say I can see my condo building from here.

With nothing left but my clothes and keys, I'm told to get up and don't turn around and run. "No mires y VETE!" they shout. I don't run. It seems silly to bother. I just walk away quickly, back toward the Friday night bustle of Restaurant Row, no wobble in my legs, no tremor in my hands, no racing heart. To be mugged on such a quiet street in front of such rarified real estate after so many years walking home at far later hours in much lousier neighborhoods seems ironic, and vapidly so. It's also that the boys looked so discombobulated when I approached them, waiting nervously between me and my half-another-block home. I nodded and offered a "Buenas," so casually that when they lunged, grabbed my shoulders, and spun me almost gracefully around, they seemed more startled by their actions than I was. It felt dumb for all involved to let a simple robbery escalate into a crime measured in degrees, so I kept repeating, "Okay. Está bien. Okay. Take it easy." They did.

Later, there will be a cascade of adrenaline, anxiously asking the police to check on my wife to make sure the boys haven't followed the home address on my driver's license. There will be shudders of the near miss, wondering if their taser actually worked, if that was an actual gun in the one kid's hand or just a stub of pipe. I will second-guess myself for months, thinking I should have turned around instead of carrying brazenly onward and saying hello to some boys leaning awkwardly against a busted-up, out-of-place Hyundai at one in the morning. Later, the police will ask what they looked like, and I'll have to answer: my height, skinny, black hair, brown skin, jeans and hoodies. Young, maybe eighteen or twenty. I'll learn that they had driven all over town looking for easy marks and, in desperation, even robbed a couple of women strolling home from a dinner out. They took the leftovers and nothing else. Later still, a detective will tell me that a Find My iPhone ping located these three boys somewhere up in Hialeah along with two other people, five undocumented bodies splitting a one-bedroom flophouse, but by the time Miami PD arrived there was no evidence left with which to charge anyone of anything.

Now, though, they've probably jumped into their car and driven off. I don't risk glancing back. I go on retracing my steps to the bar, empty-handed and alone, between luxury townhouses and luxury sedans on a cool February night. Skinny, black hair, brown skin, jeans and a hoodie. Maybe thirty-five or forty. If not for the white of my chin stubble, I might be mistaken for one of my muggers. An older brother, at least. This is the thing about living here: for the first time in my life, I really fit in. Unremarkable as rain in the rainy season, ordinary as poinciana and oleander and palm, my skin, face, and body feel more at home in Miami than they've ever been allowed to feel anywhere else in this country. It's the brownness of South Florida, its un-Americana, that I so adore. In truth, I'm more a minority here than in other towns I've called home. Weeks pass between encounters with anyone else of South Asian descent. But as far as most anyone can tell I'm indistinguishably un-white, plainly part of Miami-Dade's sunbaked one-of-us. Even the muggers here address me in Spanish.

I've rarely felt so ordinary. So accepted. In the predominantly white, Christian north, normalcy is defined and legislated by a self-satisfied majority such that the rest of us might be forgiven for feeling we're an invasive species resident in somebody else's country. Someone always comes along inquiring where I'm *really* from, the question always presented with an air of charitable curiosity, as if my inquisitor should be congratulated for paying me any mind at all. As if this nation doesn't birth brown bodies.

Miami, south of The South, has no such trouble. Not even my name tangles a tongue here where hardly anybody speaks English Only. I've been greeted in Italian, Arabic, Spanish, and Hindi. In the unironically named Mint Leaf Indian Brasserie, a few blocks from where I'm walking tonight, a desi waiter once seemed downright tickled when I answered his English with Punjabi; he then delivered my order to the kitchen staff in Spanish. This place is so contrary to what I know of America that I can't help but find it refreshing. It's a mosh of immigrants and natives born of émigrés, of refugees and retirees, hospitality and service workers, bankers and realtors, business moguls, drug moguls, celebrity moguls, tourists upon tourists upon tourists. For all its diversity and cosmopolitanism, all its exploitative development and growth, all its gaudy luxury and catastrophic poverty, all its sinister inequalities of wealth and opportunity, all of it doomed by certainties of climate change and rising seas, living here can feel like living in the hot, crowded, hyper-capitalist, globalized future—already the nation so many studies predict the United States is becoming.

In November 2016, just a few months from tonight's misadventure, majorities here in Florida and in the greater South, in concert with those in a couple of northern states I once called home, will lift a racist into the White House, his regressive platform built on a promise to wall the nation off from that fate. Those majorities fear that my bad luck this evening will be our collective misfortune. They fear that undocumented boys fleeing poverty and violence everywhere else will continue to arrive here in droves to mug and rape and murder America, and they would rather leave those boys to rot in their own brown towns. But my town is their town, and the faces of the boys who mugged me had not one flicker of villainy in them. The only thing I clearly remember of them was their bravado, the false front barely mustered against whatever hunger had driven them to this quiet street down which I happened to be walking home. I'm not a victim of their malice. I'm a victim of their desperation, which is how my neighbors' misfortunes become my own. Certainly these boys should be found and prosecuted. Certainly I feel scared and angry and violated. But hungry enough, frightened enough, hopeless enough, I might mug me too.

When the racist delivers his dark vision and his people deliver him to power, I'll feel relieved to live here among all these foreign bodies, even those of my muggers. Whatever threat or violence awaits this nation in the years ahead, none of it lurks because we permit diversity and difference to enter here. It awaits us because we permit disparity and indifference to smolder, because we seek not to correct desperation and injustice but to insulate ourselves from them. If our luxuries are worth taking, it's because we walk obliviously among those we leave wanting. But they will not leave us. They are us. In Miami, wherever you're coming from, wherever you think you're going, this is a fact that seems anxious to find you even on a quiet night when you are bothering no one, are perfectly at home in the lush and gorgeous weather.

MY PEOPLE

Weekends in our Chicago suburb, the immigrant who lived next door would hunch on a rigid wooden chair in his garage and absently watch a thirteen-inch color television whose thin antennae barely mustered the berserk picture on its screen. He would smoke upward of a pack of cigarettes a day and down a case of Heineken deliberately, quietly, alone. Beyond this, his only task those afternoons off from the ironworks was to mow the lawn, after which he happily devoted a clattering hour or two to manicuring the grass around his wife's flower beds. In spite of his evident affection for lawn care, whenever he saw me sent out by my father to mow our own lawn, he would offer a scrunched smile, untangle his Bavarian tongue, and call cheerfully in accented English, "When you finish, Jas, you come over and cut my grass too!" This became his recurring joke, and he had a variation of it no matter the season. When I trudged out to corral the autumn leaves, I would be greeted by the immigrant grinning and calling me over to clear his already tidy yard. In winter, when I was sent to shovel our driveway, he would already have tossed most of the snow from his own, but he would grin and shout through the chiseling wind, "When you finish, Jas, you come over and clean my driveway too!"

We'd befriended the immigrant and his family only a few months after moving into our house. My mother would invite them all—the immigrant and his wife, her elderly aunt, and the grown son who lived with them— over for samosas, for lamb masala, for dahl or aloo gobi. They would invite us over for steak fillets wrapped in bacon, for slaw and mashed potatoes and gravy, for pastries that should have been sold in a European bakery for two dollars an ounce. Depending on which household was grilling burgers on a given summer day, meat patties wrapped in aluminum foil would be passed one way or the other over the short chain-link fence between our gardens.

A year or so after we moved in, during one of our dinners together, the immigrant noticed the black-and-white portrait of my father's father on display in our living room. In the photograph, taken some time between the Great War and its successor, both of which he served in, my grandfather stands at attention in front of a brick wall, dark-bearded and turbaned, in full military regalia. A subedar. I never knew him. He died in 1957, when my father was only eleven, and this is my only impression of him, the one I think of when I hear the word *grandfather*. A few days after that dinner, the immigrant walked out of his garage, crossed the grass to our driveway, called to my father and me in the afternoon light, and eagerly thrust a frame toward us. It too contained a photograph of a soldier: the uncle who had raised him, also in full military regalia, standing at attention during the Second World War. Now the immigrant presented it to us. "My uncle! He was soldier too! Like *you* father," he exclaimed, leaving off the *r* in *your*. "He was in the SS!"

The immigrant beamed at this earnest offer of friendship. "Like *you* father!" he repeated in strudeled English. My father took the photograph in hand, betraying no surprise at the apparition of this soldier, this photograph that could have been pulled from a history book, a portrait of villainy. He held it gingerly. He looked into the other side of the war, paused a moment, then smiled, nodded, and said, "Yes. I see. Thank you," before handing back the frame.

In this moment, some avenue of history ended. In our driveway, an old argument evaporated. In this way, a people is born. When we in this country say *only in America*, this is what we mean.

This minor occurrence on an otherwise unremarkable day in the dull comfort of suburbia has long reminded me how complicated the question of identity is in the United States, how resistant identity can be to differentiating labels like *South Asian American* or *European American*.

The neighbor's offering was an erasure of ethnic and racial difference in favor of a shared immigrant experience. I don't imagine he was naïve. He must have understood the resentment the portrait might evoke, but he offered it anyway. After all, the immigrant's uncle, a Romanian, had been drafted unwillingly into the Nazi machine, and whatever we think of the choices he faced and the decisions he made, the elder's actions are not his heir's. When the war is over, its orphans are left to negotiate the peace.

In that moment, my father and the neighbor gathered in a better version of this country, one based on a democratic erasure of the past and the creation of a common identity. *We're in this together*, we say, even as we quarrel over the question of who exactly *we* means. In a place where nearly every language is uttered, nearly every history remembered, nearly every ancestry braided together, the answer to that question isn't obvious. I can only tell you that by the time the neighbor retired from the ironworks a decade or so later, tumors were boring through his guts undetected, and that a few years after their discovery, a few years after his stomach was removed and he withered through chemo, a few years after he had grown hairless and wan, the neighbor died. I can tell you he was a lovely guy. He was one of my people, and I miss him.

AMERICAN, INDIAN

You know why they call them Indians? Because
Columbus thought he was in India. They're called
Indians because some white guy got lost.

—Herb Stempel, *Quiz Show*

We called them American bhua and American phupher, the middle of my father's three older sisters and her husband. As the vanguard of my family's transplants to the U.S., they'd been assigned these honorifics by their nieces and nephews living then in England. American phupher arrived in Chicago for a temporary stay in the late fifties, then returned permanently with bhua in 1971. Together they raised three children while she labored in an electronics assembly plant, and he worked first as a diesel engineer for the Chicago Transit Authority and later in its managerial ranks. In their earliest years here, they would occasionally receive a phone call from a stranger who had just arrived at O'Hare on British Airways or Air India. The callers didn't speak much English, and they had no friends or family in the city; they'd simply found a payphone in the terminal, opened the directory, and dialed the number next to any name that sounded like it came from their part of the world. When these calls came in, my uncle would drive from the family's apartment in Logan Square to the airport and collect the newcomers, whether they were Punjabi, Pakistani, or Bangladeshi, whether they were Hindu, Muslim, or Sikh, and he and my aunt would host them, sometimes for months, until they had secured employment and apartment leases.

This is a kind of generosity that has been practiced by generations of immigrants to and from every part of the world. Among South Asians, such ethnic esprit de corps is captured most succinctly by the term *desi*, which Vijay Prashad defines to include those of Indian, Pakistani,

Bangladeshi, Afghani, Sri Lankan, and Nepalese descent. It isn't his invention. It's commonplace enough among my family that I know it to mean *one of us* in a manner akin to the Italian *paisan*. Derived from Sanskrit, *desi* refers to umber skin and curried English, but—like *paisan* again—its application isn't entirely seamless. Where outsiders might see homogeneity, immense internecine tensions permeate the histories of the desi peoples. Even among Indians arrived in the West from what is ostensibly a single country, there are chasms of cultural, linguistic, and religious difference that make India more like the fitful cohesion of Europe's constituent nations than anything resembling the U.S. Uniting all our tongues, gods, cultures, and bodies under a single desi banner is tribalism elevated to a continental scale, and it doesn't quite work.

Yet *desi* isn't a wrong category for us to embrace. When you live in a place that doesn't recognize differences between you and anyone who looks vaguely like you, you come to accept, even welcome, certain conflations. Partition isn't much remembered. Who assassinated whose head of state and for what reason doesn't seem to matter any longer. The cold war over Kashmir, the occupation of Amritsar, the Bangladesh Liberation War, the centuries-long history of persecution and conflict across South Asia—these are hardly known, much less understood, in the West. Here, survival matters. Wellness matters. It matters that we have each other. Growing up in Chicago in the eighties and nineties, it seemed to me that I really might be related to anyone with brown skin and a Bollywood accent. My "uncles" and "aunties" were Gujarati and Pakistani, Hindu and Muslim, Jatt Sikh and Saini. They were shopkeepers and cab drivers, laborers and tailors, professors and physicians. If it takes a village, I lived in a flourishing and richly populated one.

Still, in that village, I have long felt like a freeloader. Though I understand and speak Punjabi and can muddle through a modicum of Urdu and Hindi, though I wore kurta pajamas as a kid and can cook a few sabzis, I know little of the vastness and diversity of the desi nations. From my one visit to India, when I was four, I remember nothing but a sensation here, an image there: a water well between stalks of what might have been sugar cane, saag and corn flour roti cooking under an open sky at night, bathing in the reservoir surrounding the Golden Temple, smoke and the lingering smell of burning hanging over farm fields. This is the entirety of my first-hand reporting on a nation of over a billion people and its sixty-five thousand years of history. Like every other child of immigrants here, first-generation or fifth-, my distance, my detachment, and my ignorance make me an American.

The wide slab of the hi-fi system in my cousins' suburban living room—different aunt and uncle, different era—sat at the center of a wooden wall unit like an idol upon an altar. In a wire rack to its left stood their collection of Hindi and Punjabi records; in an identical rack to its right was their American collection, which read like Billboard's Top 100 for the eighties: Madonna, Michael Jackson, Prince, Whitney Houston, The Police, Tina Turner, Huey Lewis, David Bowie. An only child, I must have spent half my childhood sleeping over at that house, where my two teenaged cousins would ask their younger sister and me to vote on what to play next. Those records became the soundtrack to our hiding and seeking, our bedsheet tents and board games, our chattering and reading and drifting off to sleep.

The voice that suited me best was Bruce Springsteen's. I liked the gravel and strain in his singing, his grinning persona and cultivated relatability. I liked the stories his songs told and the stories he told in rambling introductions to live versions of them. They reminded me of our family. Only eight or ten years old, I knew almost nothing of New Jersey or the Rust Belt or the heartland, of Vietnam or recessions or the blue-collar whiteness his lyrics so often embrace, but our money was tight too. We lived in regular homes in working-class neighborhoods. Our parents and aunts and uncles drove aging Oldsmobiles and Fords to their jobs in factories and other unglamorous places, and no matter the long hours they put in, they never seemed to get all they deserved. Just like the people in Bruce's songs. Like Bruce, though, we seemed to be having a good time anyway, and anyway I was born in the USA, and all of this together meant his music was my music. Knowing a little more about Springsteen's politics now, I imagine he'd be fine with my overeager empathies. Knowing a lot more about America, I'm not sure the people he sings about would.

The people he sings about are generally counted among the nebulous "white working class" whose political whims have alternately obsessed and held hostage the news media since the election of our current president in 2016. People who fit that description are corralled into televised focus groups and town halls, scrutinized and analyzed in print and in films and on podcasts, polled and pandered to by politicians of every persuasion—and what materializes is a portrait of a mostly decent but fearful people who fervently believe their own legends. They're devoted to this land they believe is their land: a place discovered, settled, tamed, and civilized by ancestors who carved their pale faces into the indifferent mountains, who settled the "wild" West and built the railroad, who won the wars and spiked their banner into the oblivious moon. They're proud of their folklore, and their pride makes them certain they deserve more than they've already taken. It allows some of them to imagine this country as an ethno-theocracy built by and for the white imagination, delivered unto them by a white god and a white messiah.

In this version of events, I have long felt like an interloper, my family and I counted among the invasives inundating the American homeland, diluting its religious and ethnic culture, swallowing up its jobs and resources—and we're only one breaker among several, arriving endlessly from so many "shithole countries" to deluge these shores. To celebrate the relentless advance of European-born settlers as evidence of a pioneer spirit while denigrating the progress of brown migrants here as an invasion is a bald hypocrisy, but the colonizer's view of American history put the supremacy in whiteness long ago. That history—impressed even upon liberal lions like Springsteen—reflexively casts one people as prototypical, authentic, and heroic while dismissing the rest of us as outsiders to the "real" America: that of the focus group, the media narrative, the rock anthem and grammar school pageant. And so, like every other child born of brown immigrants, first-generation or fifth-, my difference keeps me detached and at a distance. My skin makes me an Indian.

*   *   *

Dots, not feathers, the other kids cracked in school, even though in my family's part of the old country you see mostly turbans and chunis, not bindis. That a single word can conflate the descendants of one continent's achingly ancient civilizations with those of another, half a planet away, is evidence of colonialism's continued hold on the American imagination. Desis, of course, have little in common with North American "Indians" beyond the depth of our histories and the diversity among our peoples. But politicians, folk historians, and Americans who proudly recast exploitative expansionism as noble and civilizing have no need for any such distinctions. Our textbooks celebrate Columbus, Daniel Boone, Lewis, Clark, and every manifestly destined land-grabber who followed as trailblazers boldly claiming uncharted territories. In this telling, America is a nation of humble pioneers confronting brutal savages, a nation of industrious homesteaders terrorized by interloping raiders, a nation of—yes—cowboys versus Indians.

I remember these lessons from grammar school, their uninterrogated heroism. They are what we mean when we say *Americana*, and they admit no responsibility for the genocides committed here. They offer no reparations for slavery. They deliver no correction to the existential threats all our technology and growth and bellicosity have wrought on the planet. They only allow the heirs of colonial power to continue laying claim to this country's historical successes while laying the blame for its failings elsewhere. And so those heirs become a burden for the rest of us. Their self-importance is our burden. Their oblivion is our burden. Their fear and anger over any challenge to their preferred narrative are our burden. Sooner or later, the question confronting the desi arrived in the U.S. is whether or not we will accept their version of history, whether we will cast our lot with the Indians or with the cowboys.

My family gathers in December 2012 for a birthday party at a cousin's house—different cousin, different era— bringing together three generations of auto mechanics and physicians, laborers and homemakers, middle managers and entrepreneurs, professors and retirees. Observant Sikhs, casual Sikhs, and those of us who claim no religion at all. In an election year, it's unsurprising that our conversation turns to politics, but in the familiarity of this space, I'm startled to hear some of my elder relatives expressing so much anger about the state of the nation and directing their vitriol at President Obama. Some who barely speak English complain that blacks and Latinos are coming for their jobs. Some complain that other minorities, even those arriving from the desi homelands, are guilty of exploiting the same social safety net from which they themselves benefit. Too many, they claim, are coming here and straining our resources, and they lay all of this at the feet of our first black president.

I'm less startled, at another gathering four years later, to learn that these same relatives are unified in their support of candidate Trump. They too want to see America made great again, in spite of the fact that they themselves, several of them bearded and turbaned, have had their homes in well-off suburbs and exurbs hatefully vandalized or riddled by the bullets of xenophobes. They support Trump's every regressive diatribe in spite of the fact that they've benefited from affirmative action and unemployment, from social security protections they now believe are too economically burdensome, from the very immigration policies they now support ending. They align themselves with the same bigoted, jingoist inclinations that would have them barred or deported from here. They speak their allegiance in Punjabi. When other members of the family challenge them, not one is willing to admit the hypocrisy or absurdity in all of this. They have another version of history in mind.

It isn't that any of them are daft enough to mistake themselves for white. It's that an exclusionary and supremacist mindset doesn't belong to the white imagination alone. It is possible for even the brown immigrant to begin to believe in his own triumphal legend: that he set out as a noble explorer and made his way, made a home for himself, that he owes nobody anything for his achievement, and that anyone arriving after him poses a threat to his own hold on resources and opportunity. Decent and devoted to this nation as he might be, he too can grow fearful and eager to blame anyone else for his misfortunes. He too can believe he deserves more than he's already taken. He doesn't have to mistake himself for a European in order to wish to be identified with white America rather than black or brown or native America. He too can simply want to be on the side of power. He too can mistake the aggressor for the hero and adopt the aggressor's values as his own. He too can betray the marginalized and the subjugated who need him most. This is how the turbaned desi comes to ally himself with white supremacists, how he becomes for someone else the very burden he wishes to escape.

This is the Indian taking the side of the cowboys, and that this is even possible ought to demonstrate how utterly invented race is, how incidental the *white* in white supremacy. The supremacist imagination is bigger than race. It merely invents race, over and over, as a means of claiming and clinging to power. Racism is not ignorant or oblivious: racism is willful. Where it is practiced, every manner of revisionism and contradiction required to preserve supremacy, every hypocrisy and absurdity, will follow. This is how the self-proclaimed greatest nation on Earth can also clamor to be made great again, how the leader of the free world can imprison children at our borders, how a nation of immigrants can turn away those tired refugees yearning to breathe free.

When my American phupher died in his sleep of a heart attack in 1997, hundreds gathered in mourning at his funeral. Just as many paid their respects after my American bhua's passing in 2018. If their example in this country is instructive of anything, it's that there's an answer to America above and beyond exclusionary thinking. Had they turned their backs on those arriving after them, had they kept for themselves alone whatever progress they made, they may well have thrived here, but they would have done so in isolation, forever afraid that someone would come along to take whatever they were hungrily protecting. They didn't do that. They chose generosity. They chose solidarity. They showed—and the desi experience writ large shows—that allegiance and community are possible even among those who would be strangers or enemies elsewhere.

WHITE WEDDING

My wife worries I married the wrong person. Through our patio doors, the facades of downtown Miami glint orange against a purpling eastern sky. In five years, our home has rarely been darkened by conflict or drama. We watch *This Old House* or *Forged in Fire* over the week's leftovers. We go for containers at the Container Store, for books at Books & Books. We have movie quotes and fart jokes and a life in writing and reading between us. Still, she wonders sometimes whether I should be with somebody else, whether my parents would have been happier if I'd kept to their traditions and been matched and married to a desi, preferably Punjabi, Sikh, educated, and gainfully employed, preferably attractive, humble, and from an affable family. I did not keep to their traditions. I made my own. I chose quoting *Ghostbusters* and *Quiz Show* over bourbons and Dirty Shirleys. I chose reluctantly agreeing to vegan sloppy joes while Miss Marple or Nick Charles nabs another old-timey murder suspect. I chose listening quietly to *Radiolab* for half of a long drive and erupting into frenetic conversation about the political legacy of Ruth Bader Ginsberg or meat allergies born of tick bites or worldbuilding in science fiction for the other half. I chose to marry a white woman. I chose the snort of her laughter, the random bouts of her New England accent, her ludicrous humor. She chose my quirks and my neuroses, my every flaw and saving grace. We chose the comfort of our commonalities, the thrill of our differences, and together we made a new family. Now our baby is napping in the other room, the storms of late afternoon giving way to the radiance of early evening. The seasons turn and return, regretting nothing.

*   *   *

Throughout my twenties and thirties, my mother would inquire, delicately but insistently, when I might marry. After dinner during visits home, my father would half-jokingly demand a grandchild. Both would from time to time tell me that an aunt or another relation had friends somewhere in Ontario or Wisconsin or England with a daughter about my age. *She's studying to be a pharmacist*, they might say. *You only need to send an email, maybe talk on the phone. No commitment. Just getting to know each other.*

Match marriage is predicated on the idea that there is a comfort among your own kind that can't be replicated among others, and it motivates desi families to deploy their social networks, both real and virtual, to assemble a raft of prospective spouses for their children. The suitability of those prospects is determined above all by shared religious, linguistic, regional, and caste backgrounds. Equivalent education levels and earning potentials are almost as critical, followed by relative attractiveness and mutual interests. The process assumes that marriages between similar people tend to work out better than marriages between dissimilar people, and that commonalities of culture, language, and background can serve as bulwarks against the almost inarticulable discomfort of two families integrating, their awkward labor of getting along.

With a wave of the hand or a roll of the eyes, I'd parry my parents' gambits at fixing me up for life with a stranger. (It was never clear whether the women in question had any interest in marrying or even knowing me, and I suspect that in their own post-dinner conversations in England or Wisconsin or Ontario those women were rolling their eyes with equal irritation.) I was ambivalent about marriage in the first place, and match marriage especially struck me as an affront to my autonomy. If I ever changed my mind about commitment, I insisted, it would be out of love.

And love is a phenomenon attributed almost exclusively, in the Western imagination, to serendipity. Countless pop songs, rom-coms, and sitcoms tell us that love is inadvertent as it is inescapable, that lifelong partnerships are gifted to those of us who need them most when we demand them least. It just sort of *happens* if we're willing to embrace unlikely people in unlikely places, especially those who initially appear, if only superficially, to be our opposites. Serendipity absolves us of our agency even as these stories insist, paradoxically, that nobody can predict or dictate whom we should be with, that love has nothing to do with race or culture or socioeconomic position. Serendipity assumes that we can overcome disparities in these categories and most any other. I learned to believe in that happy ending. I wanted it for myself, even as my parents feared so much serendipity would lure me away from my own kind and into the arms of an American.

But my wife is my own kind, and it's precisely because she still worries about all of this, will bring it up while we're eating reheated spaghetti and watching PBS, that we've never had any trouble getting along. When she wonders whether I married the wrong person, it's not that she really believes I should be with somebody else; it's that she earnestly cares about my mother and father and knows how much their culture means to them, how eager they are for her to embrace that culture and its way of living, its language and cuisine and traditions. It's that she's genuinely concerned that I didn't meet a desi woman, on my own or via family mediation, if only to keep these kind, sincere, inordinately generous people happy.

Knowing that I moved so decisively and so permanently away from my parents' culture does sometimes make me feel like I betrayed them, like I disregarded their happiness and turned my back on that generosity. I did what I wanted without fully considering where my wanting came from, without feeling accountable for how it might affect them. If I had long understood that my desires would challenge theirs, a lifetime of Western television, music, and literature only affirmed that this was how it should be—that desire is meant to topple convention. Love is egalitarian and cool; parents are not. And yet my marriage, and the other relationships that preceded it, might be evidence that those successes of chemistry and timing are never quite so serendipitous as our stories about love suggest, that attraction and passion are secondary to ethnicity, race, and culture rather than the other way around. That in making the choices I made, I acted against my mother and father, against myself and our people.

In the Western view, the idea that your father's older sister should find you a spouse somewhere in Toronto or Milwaukee or Wolverhampton based on little more than your age, education, physical attributes, and earning potential feels bizarrely transactional, as if children were chattel. Worse, it's indifferent to the desires of the individual—which is true to a reprehensible degree for women pressured into such marriages, and even more so for queer and transgender people whose realities aren't remotely acknowledged by the practice. Yet the criteria involved in match and arranged marriage aren't wholly different, in the end, from those used by our friends setting us up with someone they know based on little more than our confessed preferences and personal histories, nor are they even so different from the surveys and algorithms on which dating websites base their matchmaking. If family fix-ups seem foreign, it's only because local context has taught us that friends, tech companies, and random chance understand our desires better than kin do.

So, while almost all of my many cousins agreed to match marriages and found long-lasting relationships, I rejected that tack in favor of the tried and true hope of locking eyes with someone across a bar or a bookstore or the produce aisle, wherever Hugh Grant or Meg Ryan seemed to have had some luck. I never did think it odd that the women I kept meeting in such places had little connection to or knowledge of my family's culture. Almost all of them were white, and I attributed this to shared interests, to career, to lifestyle, to commonality of education and location, even though these commonalities were already baked into middle-class mainstream American culture and its bias against outsiders. I didn't have an overt preference for white women, but I did have preferences for many of the things that have for decades been guarded by and for white people. I attributed this to serendipity too.

* * *

Weirdly, my marriage coincided with a sudden uptick in media depictions of brown-white romance. Exhilarating as it might be to see desi men turning up in mainstream pop culture, especially in leading roles, neither I nor my wife can say we like *Master of None* or *Meet the Patels* or *The Big Sick* very much. We're disappointed by the lack of innovation beyond the casting of a brown guy in the role of charming but hapless hero, and by the general exclusion of women of color except as props. Desi women in particular become grotesques representing the staid and dullard culture of the old world, obstacles for the brown leading men to step on and around in an effort to avoid the same dehumanized fate.

White women, meanwhile, embodying a Westernized version of love, become a different sort of prop, one bound up in the brown boy's efforts at assimilation. As the stories go, he denies what he must in order to fit into his white lover's worldview, and when he falters she is empowered to forgive and accept him among the family and friends who constitute her own kind. Her efforts are at absolving his strangeness; his are at altering what is deemed strange, including otherwise unremarkable cultural norms such as familial obligation, non-Christian faith, and conventions like match marriage. The desi protagonist's willingness to engage in this dynamic suggests that being welcomed into homes and beds and romantic imaginations that have long excluded him is worth his supplication, while also affirming that being accepted into the American mainstream requires his participation in its disdain for those who are like him, those he no longer wishes to be like.

Growing up, I didn't see many people who looked like me on television. Where South Asians did appear in pop culture, they tended to arrive as caricatures, born of a narrative need for a villain, a fool, the fulfillment of a passing fancy. Our exclusion felt normal, so much so that it eventually became easy enough to mistake tokenization for inclusion. *I have a thing for Indian guys*, women have said to me. *Indian chicks are hot*, men have said to me. It's a kind of flattery that feels like want, a lusty desire that can be taken for acceptance, but it is neither of those. White people don't say such things about other white people. Nobody says this about their own kind. They say it about those they find exotic: the token made fetish.

Yet people of color who appear where they aren't expected are often lionized as part of a racial vanguard, as if their mere presence brings us one step nearer to the misguided dream of a colorblind America. As much as any vanguard represents progress, these trailblazers aren't evidence of a nation's sudden embrace of diversity so much as evidence of the majority's self-congratulatory tolerance of it. The vanguard is celebrated for demonstrating that we're all alike, when what it actually demonstrates is that brown and black people can fight alongside white people, can be friends with white people, can sometimes even fall in love with white people. In this, our pipe dream of a post-racial future has everything to do with the endorsement and preservation of existing hierarchies of race. And because it's a future that happens to include depictions of marriages like my own, I can be cast as part of a vanguard even as I question whether I've been assimilated against myself, whether I'm an infiltrator or a traitor.

Assimilation asks immigrants and their offspring to learn and adhere to the mores of the dominant culture for the greater good. This is sold to us as unit cohesion on a national scale, but it neglects the possibility that the entrant might have something better on offer. In the absence of that possibility, the majority is authorized, by little more than its numbers, to demean and ostracize any outsider who fails to resemble it sufficiently, who doesn't value what it values; any criticism leveled against the mainstream is rejected as ingratitude or uppity agitation or the feeble badgering of so many snowflakes. For the racial minority in a country that reflexively claims a white Christian identity, total assimilation is impossible and failure isn't an option. This nation will surveil us, deport us, imprison us, and shoot us in the street for the simple fact that we don't affirm its existing sense of normalcy, and it will blame its actions on our shortcomings rather than its own.

But after we change our clothes, our hair, our language and affect, after we've changed everything except our faces and bodies, we're offered another means to demonstrate our fealty: we can accept the opportunity to enact whiteness, to join its domineering majority and rehearse its performance of racism, misogyny, and supremacy. This is one method for becoming a model minority. In agreeing to this, you might feel you've surpassed tokenization, been granted sincere acceptance, when what you've actually been given is a kiss on the head for your capitulation.

I did go out with some desi women and women of other backgrounds during my years drifting around the dating pool, and those dates didn't lead to marriage for the same prosaic reasons most dates and relationships don't lead to marriage. Even so, I mostly dated white women, and I mostly kept my relationships secret from my family. I told myself my covertness was in the interest of allaying their fears over my increasing Americanization—that I wanted to protect them from worry—but there is both shame and self-regard in hiding. My shame was rooted in my alignment with a mainstream that dismisses the validity of outsiders like my parents; my self-regard was in trusting my own judgment over my family's, over that of the hundreds of millions of people in South Asia and abroad who live and love and thrive by the trusted and enduring mores of our collective culture. The arrogance in the latter is astonishing, which might make it the most American thing about me.

Not everyone makes this choice. For those of us who do, the customs of our families may feel outmoded, and we may find love outside of them, but this doesn't mean we're entirely vindicated by our good fortune. Something still keeps us apart from the people we are nearest to, something more than happenstance, more than kismet. Our desires are corrupted by our participation in the dominant culture. That culture teaches us to make its values our values and to carry them above every other, so when we're given the choice we choose against our own.

Or maybe this is simply what it means to be in the minority. Maybe finding others who are truly like us, who are not only suitable by the criteria of our ancestral cultures but who also share our passions, who appreciate our quirks and flaws and happen to be in the right places at the right times, is almost impossible. So we love the ones we're with. If we have to change and deny ourselves in ways the majority never does, maybe this is just the cost of admission. Almost every desi woman I ever went out with eventually married a white person too.

But my wife has also been asked to change: to grapple with a new language and culture, to interrogate her own upbringing, to reckon with the exclusionary values of her heritage even as she's confronted with the regressive gender dynamics and bigotries of mine. She's been asked to embrace people who harbor only thinly veiled suspicions of her name, background, and skin color. Indeed, what those recent movies and shows do get right is that xenophobia is a swinging door. Some desi parents' fear of their children marrying white people runs just as deep as any white fear of color, and their misgivings aren't reserved for whiteness alone: there is viciously intolerant opposition among many of our elders to their offspring marrying into other racial or ethnic minorities, even marrying into other religions, castes, and regions of South Asia. This isn't just obvious bigotry; it's also contradictory. It holds culture as intrinsic to race and place of origin while also holding that culture can be corrupted by embracing what's foreign. If the former is true, the latter shouldn't be a threat; if the latter is possible, culture is no more fundamental than a hairstyle. Ironically, the resistance to intermarriage is strikingly similar to the Western demand for our assimilation: that we should arrive here and adapt without transforming completely is only an inverse articulation of the notion that we are welcome in this country so long as we don't disrupt or change it too greatly.

Our elders, of course, are no less fervent in their perspectives than America is in its own. But while it has long owed its global appeal to its democratic freedoms, its principles of equality and justice, and its technological and cultural achievements, this nation is exceptional for other reasons as well. Its militarism and exploitative economic expansions, its excesses and frivolity, its bigotry and arrogance and violence. And since these negative associations accrue to the white identity that the U.S. mass-markets through its entertainment and politics, an immigrant may well conclude that the white American mainstream is selfish, materialist, promiscuous, addicted to booze and drugs and junk food, trigger-happy and belligerently intolerant of outsiders. Immigrants, it turns out, can stereotype too. Between this and the wrath they regularly face from that portion of white America that actually does hate them, our parents have little desire to surrender their children to such a people. When they fear that whiteness will seduce us with the promise of love, at the cost of our devotion to them and their culture, our elders are right to panic.

This too is why my wife worries I married the wrong person. Not because she doesn't feel as deeply for me as I do for her, but because of the weight of my family's distrust of those who look like her, those who share her background and upbringing—because of their reflexive mistrust of her kind. There might be some measure of poetic justice in her being forced to bear the burden of whiteness in this way, but my parents and my wife aren't hostile factions in an intractable war of acculturation. They're my family, and I want more than justice for them. I want joy.

For all I share with my wife—language, humor, learning, cultural reference, and mutual attraction—our families don't have much in common beyond affability. There is no history or tradition between them. This has nothing to do with race, except for the way race becomes shorthand for all we don't have in common. My wife's family is white and mine is not, so there is the culture of her people and the culture of my people, and there is the worry that these two cultures can't be reconciled: that there will always be something—some lingering, unspoken discomfort, some conflict or regret—keeping them and us apart.

That thing is the fact that the call to assimilation isn't colorblind. We will continue to have white nationalists marching in our streets, to have elected officials caught in blackface or spouting slurs into hot mics, to have law enforcement agencies committing violence against people they should protect, for as long as the American way makes cultural capitulation a prerequisite to national harmony, for as long as American white-ness regards its preference for itself as unremarkable, for as long as it requires others to accept its biases as the standard of normalcy. We are right to worry. If it's harmony and equality we're after, we should remember that equality between alike things is a tautological sham. Besides which it's boring. Actual equality is predicated on difference, on mutual respect between dissimilar people—as in a marriage. And as in a marriage, our nation will be whole only when we expect, admire, and desire differences between us, not because serendipity or history arranged it, but because we know we are not the same and want each other anyway.

When they come visit us and their grandson now, my mother and father know I didn't leave my heritage at the Florida courthouse where I married my wife. They adore their daughter—there is no *-in-law* when they address her—and they know that the singular baby we've brought into the world wouldn't exist if all of us weren't in this together.

What we don't know yet is what any of this will mean for our son. I don't know whether my minority will live on in him as my wife's whiteness is overwritten, or the other way around. I think sometimes of Anne Dunham, the white woman from Kansas whose child became the first black president of the United States, of how those people who lived by the one-drop rule probably didn't foresee their own racist legacy dying by it. I don't know how often our child will be held up as evidence of the successful integration of peoples and cultures in the U.S. without anyone acknowledging just how fraught and fucked up that integration was. I don't know what of himself he will be asked to alter or elide or deny. I know only that culture isn't a thing we can bestow or force upon him. His culture will be something he creates, and when he does, I hope he and his people can forgive and correct what we got wrong. It's a lot to ask of them, but if we ask too much of the future, it's because we've asked too little of ourselves.

CODA

Those who knew
what this was all about
must make way for those
who know little.
And less than that.
And at last nothing less than nothing.
> —*Wisława Symborska, "The End and the*
> *Beginning" (tr. Stanisław Barańczak and*
> *Clare Cavanagh)*

New Year's Eve, 2018, 11:04 p.m., our son is fitfully asleep in his bassinet, his mother in bed beside him reading on her phone, and here on our balcony the amateur fireworks over Miami are erupting erratic and loud, threatening in their wobbly randomness, threatening in their proximity. Proximity puts the dread in every threat, but tonight I'm thinking of distance. In another hour or so, a probe will speed past a tiny, icy body at the outskirts of the solar system, then hurtle onward for eons. For all that will transpire in that ever after, however arbitrary and erroneous my perception of time might be, it will never be the year of my son's birth again—2018. His year. Strange how its reality will never occupy his mind: not its exhaustions or joys, not its politics or its memes, not its rhythms or light or anger. It will remain just beyond his recollection, and here in its waning hour we're hurtling out of, I'm devastated that it will never be this year again.

I'm trying now to preserve this iota so that he and his mother and I will know it was real, that once we were in this moment together, in this home where I proposed to her, where he was conceived, where her labor began, where he's fitful and fussing even now. So we will know it was wonderful. I'm trying to preserve it, but this moment will not still itself from becoming the next one. Soon his words will come, his first and his second and then thousands more, in one language and in others. The skyline will revise itself with new architecture. The city and nation will complicate themselves with new bodies until the ocean encroaches and rewrites all our coast-lines. We'll go away. Others will arrive. America will end. But right now the night is gunpowder smoke and haze, warm and damp so that the air conditioning chills my skin when I step inside to shiver in the half-light. There is no argument or complication here. There is only a body writing. Against time. In its own quaint space. Without apology.

Grateful acknowledgment to the editors at the following venues where versions of these essays appeared in earlier drafts:

Empathy for the Devil: *The State* (Dubai), Issue 1, March 2012

Writing Like a White Guy: *Poetry Foundation dot com*, November 2011; *Language: A Reader for Writers*, Oxford University Press, 2013; *A Sense of Regard: Essays on Poetry and Race*, University of Georgia Press, 2015; *The Norton Reader*, 14th edition, W.W. Norton, 2016

Color Coded: *Poetry Foundation dot com*, May 2016

What I Tell Them: *Poets on Teaching*, University of Iowa Press, 2010; *CREDO: An Anthology of Manifestos and Sourcebook for Creative Writing*, Cambridge Writers' Workshop and C&R Press, 2018

The Writing Class: *Poetry Foundation dot com*, November 2014

Foreign and Domestic: *Here: 20 Writers of Color on the New South*, Hub City Writers Project, 2020

My People: excerpted from "Tribe," *Himal Southasian*, Vol. 26, No. 1: "Are We Sure About India?" 2013

Thank you

with all my enduring love and respect to my parents for this life and everything in it

to Auntie, Uncle, Panj, Paj, and Pop without whom I am not me

to all my enormous family by blood, by heritage, or by great fortune

to Kathleen and Thomas Walsh for being part of that family and welcoming me with love and generosity into your own

to those gone and remembered in these essays

to the many, many editors along the way, but first and foremost to Joshua Marie Wilkinson, Patrick Culliton, Travis Nichols, and to the Poetry Foundation where all this essaying began

to Amanda Uhle, Sunra Thompson, and McSweeney's for taking such extraordinary care in the making of this book

to Michelle Kuo and Albert Wu for the generosity of your time and your indispensable thoughts on all of this to Sarah Manguso for your guidance and your confidence precisely when I needed both most

to Ian Bonaparte for your kind heart and your earnest partnership in this endeavor

to Daniel Levin Becker who willed this book into being. It simply wouldn't exist without you, and for all your intelligence, diligence, persistence, and humor, it's as much yours now as it is mine. All the O'Tacos you can eat and any related accoutrements are on me forever and always

to Robyn for this life and everything in it. Without you, I am not me. Without you, none of it matters. Oooma.

Jaswinder Bolina is author of the poetry collections *The 44th of July*, *Phantom Camera*, and *Carrier Wave*, and of the digital chapbook *The Tallest Building in America*. His essays and poems have appeared widely in the U.S. and abroad and have been included in anthologies such as *The Best American Poetry* and *The Norton Reader*. He teaches on the faculty of the MFA Program in Creative Writing at the University of Miami.